Trampoline

GYMNASTICS GOALBOOK

© Dream Co Publishing 2020. ISBN 978-0-9951317-7-4

Sports club bulk orders: orders@dreamcomedia.nz

Image credit: BlueRingMedia/Shutterstock.com

Contents:

Info	page 1
Encouraging quotes	page 2
Yearly Training Goals	page 4
Training Goals	page 8
Competition Goals	page 64

Gymnastics Info:

Name: _____

Age: _____

Level: _____

Club: _____

Coach/es: _____

Favourite skill/s: _____

_____

Favourite trampoline event/s: _____

_____

Favourite Olympic gymnast: _____

_____

Favourite leotard colour: _____

Inspirational words or quotes:

Inspirational words or quotes:

My Yearly Training Goals:

Date: _____

_____
_____
_____
_____
_____
_____
_____
_____
_____
_____
_____
_____
_____
_____

 You can do it!

My Yearly Training Outcomes:

Date: _____

_____
_____
_____
_____
_____
_____
_____
_____
_____
_____
_____
_____
_____
_____
_____

 Go for gold!

My Yearly Training Goals:

Date: _____

_____
_____
_____
_____
_____
_____
_____
_____
_____
_____
_____
_____
_____

♡ *Dreams are possible.* ♡

My Yearly Training Outcomes:

Date: _____

_____
_____
_____
_____
_____
_____
_____
_____
_____
_____
_____
_____
_____
_____
_____
_____

♡ *Flipping out is fun!* ♡

My Training Goals:

Date: _____

_____
_____
_____
_____
_____
_____
_____
_____
_____
_____
_____
_____
_____
_____
_____
_____
_____

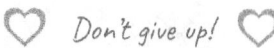

Don't give up!

My Training Outcomes:

Date: _____

_____
_____
_____
_____
_____
_____
_____
_____
_____
_____
_____
_____
_____
_____
_____
_____
_____

 Train like a champion.

My Training Goals:

Date: _____

_____
_____
_____
_____
_____
_____
_____
_____
_____
_____
_____
_____
_____
_____
_____
_____

♡ *Aim high!* ♡

My Training Outcomes:

Date: _____

_____
_____
_____
_____
_____
_____
_____
_____
_____
_____
_____
_____
_____
_____
_____
_____

My Training Goals:

Date: _____

_____
_____
_____
_____
_____
_____
_____
_____
_____
_____
_____
_____
_____
_____
_____
_____
_____

 If you don't try – you won't know what you're actually capable of.

My Training Outcomes:

Date: _____

_____
_____
_____
_____
_____
_____
_____
_____
_____
_____
_____
_____
_____
_____
_____
_____

♡ *You got this!* ♡

My Training Goals:

Date: _____

_____
_____
_____
_____
_____
_____
_____
_____
_____
_____
_____
_____
_____
_____
_____
_____

 You're amazing.

My Training Outcomes:

Date: _____

_____
_____
_____
_____
_____
_____
_____
_____
_____
_____
_____
_____
_____
_____
_____
_____
_____

♡ *Believe – achieve.* ♡

My Training Goals:

Date: _____

_____
_____
_____
_____
_____
_____
_____
_____
_____
_____
_____
_____
_____
_____
_____
_____

♡ ...it's a gymnast thing. ♡

My Training Outcomes:

Date: _____

_____
_____
_____
_____
_____
_____
_____
_____
_____
_____
_____
_____
_____
_____
_____
_____

♡ *Be flexible, be strong. And smile!* ♡

My Training Goals:

Date: _____

_____
_____
_____
_____
_____
_____
_____
_____
_____
_____
_____
_____
_____
_____
_____
_____
_____

You can do it!

My Training Outcomes:

Date: _____

_____
_____
_____
_____
_____
_____
_____
_____
_____
_____
_____
_____
_____
_____
_____
_____
_____

 Go for gold!

My Training Goals:

Date: _____

_____
_____
_____
_____
_____
_____
_____
_____
_____
_____
_____
_____
_____
_____
_____
_____

 *Dreams are possible.*

My Training Outcomes:

Date: _____

Flipping out is fun!

My Training Goals:

Date: _____

_____
_____
_____
_____
_____
_____
_____
_____
_____
_____
_____
_____
_____
_____
_____

♡ *Don't give up!* ♡

My Training Outcomes:

Date: _____

_____
_____
_____
_____
_____
_____
_____
_____
_____
_____
_____
_____
_____
_____
_____
_____
_____

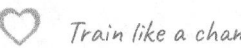

Train like a champion.

My Training Goals:

Date: _____

_____
_____
_____
_____
_____
_____
_____
_____
_____
_____
_____
_____
_____
_____
_____

 Aim high!

My Training Outcomes:

Date: _____

You're a star!

My Training Goals:

Date: _____

_____
_____
_____
_____
_____
_____
_____
_____
_____
_____
_____
_____
_____
_____
_____
_____
_____

♡ *Trampolining counts as flying.* ♡

My Training Outcomes:

Date: _____

_____
_____
_____
_____
_____
_____
_____
_____
_____
_____
_____
_____
_____
_____
_____

♡ *I love gymnastics!* ♡

My Training Goals:

Date: _____

_____
_____
_____
_____
_____
_____
_____
_____
_____
_____
_____
_____
_____
_____
_____
_____

 If you don't try – you won't know what you're actually capable of.

My Training Outcomes:

Date: _____

_____
_____
_____
_____
_____
_____
_____
_____
_____
_____
_____
_____
_____
_____
_____

You got this!

My Training Goals:

Date: _____

_____
_____
_____
_____
_____
_____
_____
_____
_____
_____
_____
_____
_____
_____

 Trampolining is the best!

My Training Outcomes:

Date: _____

_____
_____
_____
_____
_____
_____
_____
_____
_____
_____
_____
_____
_____
_____
_____
_____
_____

♡ *Don't forget to have fun.* ♡

My Training Goals:

Date: _____

_____
_____
_____
_____
_____
_____
_____
_____
_____
_____
_____
_____
_____
_____

♡ *Run towards a challenge, not away from it.* ♡

My Training Outcomes:

Date: _____

_____

_____

_____

_____

_____

_____

_____

_____

_____

_____

_____

_____

_____

_____

♡ *Fly like an eagle.* ♡

My Training Goals:

Date: _____

_____
_____
_____
_____
_____
_____
_____
_____
_____
_____
_____
_____
_____
_____
_____

You're amazing.

My Training Outcomes:

Date: _____

_____
_____
_____
_____
_____
_____
_____
_____
_____
_____
_____
_____
_____
_____
_____
_____
_____

♡ *Believe – achieve.* ♡

My Training Goals:

Date: _____

_____
_____
_____
_____
_____
_____
_____
_____
_____
_____
_____
_____
_____
_____
_____

♡ ...it's a gymnast thing. ♡

My Training Outcomes:

Date: _____

_____
_____
_____
_____
_____
_____
_____
_____
_____
_____
_____
_____
_____
_____
_____

♡ *Be flexible, be strong. And smile!* ♡

My Training Goals:

Date: _____

_____
_____
_____
_____
_____
_____
_____
_____
_____
_____
_____
_____
_____
_____
_____
_____

 You can do it!

My Training Outcomes:

Date: _____

_____
_____
_____
_____
_____
_____
_____
_____
_____
_____
_____
_____
_____
_____
_____

Go for gold!

My Training Goals:

Date: _____

_____
_____
_____
_____
_____
_____
_____
_____
_____
_____
_____
_____
_____
_____
_____
_____

 Dreams are possible.

My Training Outcomes:

Date: _____

_____
_____
_____
_____
_____
_____
_____
_____
_____
_____
_____
_____
_____
_____
_____
_____
_____

♡ *Flipping out is fun!* ♡

My Training Goals:

Date: _____

_____
_____
_____
_____
_____
_____
_____
_____
_____
_____
_____
_____
_____
_____
_____

♡ *Don't give up!* ♡

My Training Outcomes:

Date: _____

_____
_____
_____
_____
_____
_____
_____
_____
_____
_____
_____
_____
_____
_____
_____

 *Train like a champion.*

My Training Goals:

Date: _____

_____
_____
_____
_____
_____
_____
_____
_____
_____
_____
_____
_____
_____
_____
_____

 Aim high!

My Training Outcomes:

Date: _____

_____
_____
_____
_____
_____
_____
_____
_____
_____
_____
_____
_____
_____
_____
_____
_____
_____

 *You're a star!*

My Training Goals:

Date: _____

_____
_____
_____
_____
_____
_____
_____
_____
_____
_____
_____
_____
_____
_____
_____
_____
_____

♡ *Trampolining counts as flying.* ♡

My Training Outcomes:

Date: _____

_____
_____
_____
_____
_____
_____
_____
_____
_____
_____
_____
_____
_____
_____
_____
_____
_____

♡ *I love trampolining!* ♡

My Training Goals:

Date: _____

_____
_____
_____
_____
_____
_____
_____
_____
_____
_____
_____
_____
_____
_____
_____
_____

 If you don't try – you won't know what you're actually capable of.

My Training Outcomes:

Date: _____

_____
_____
_____
_____
_____
_____
_____
_____
_____
_____
_____
_____
_____
_____
_____
_____

♡ *You got this!* ♡

My Training Goals:

Date: _____

_____
_____
_____
_____
_____
_____
_____
_____
_____
_____
_____
_____
_____
_____
_____

♡ *Trampolining is the best!* ♡

My Training Outcomes:

Date: _____

_____
_____
_____
_____
_____
_____
_____
_____
_____
_____
_____
_____
_____
_____
_____

♡ *Don't forget to have fun.* ♡

My Training Goals:

Date: _____

_____
_____
_____
_____
_____
_____
_____
_____
_____
_____
_____
_____
_____
_____
_____
_____
_____

 Run towards a challenge, not away from it.

My Training Outcomes:

Date: _____

_____
_____
_____
_____
_____
_____
_____
_____
_____
_____
_____
_____
_____
_____
_____

♡ *Trampolining counts as flying.* ♡

My Training Goals:

Date: _____

_____
_____
_____
_____
_____
_____
_____
_____
_____
_____
_____
_____
_____
_____
_____
_____
_____

♡ *You're amazing.* ♡

My Training Outcomes:

Date: _____

_____
_____
_____
_____
_____
_____
_____
_____
_____
_____
_____
_____
_____
_____
_____
_____
_____

♡ *Believe – achieve.* ♡

My Training Goals:

Date: _____

_____
_____
_____
_____
_____
_____
_____
_____
_____
_____
_____
_____
_____
_____
_____

♡ ...it's a gymnast thing. ♡

My Training Outcomes:

Date: _____

_____
_____
_____
_____
_____
_____
_____
_____
_____
_____
_____
_____
_____
_____
_____

♡ *Be flexible, be strong. And smile!* ♡

My Training Goals:

Date: _____

_____
_____
_____
_____
_____
_____
_____
_____
_____
_____
_____
_____
_____
_____
_____
_____

 You can do it!

My Training Outcomes:

Date: _____

_____
_____
_____
_____
_____
_____
_____
_____
_____
_____
_____
_____
_____
_____
_____
_____

 Go for gold!

My Training Goals:

Date: _____

_____
_____
_____
_____
_____
_____
_____
_____
_____
_____
_____
_____
_____
_____
_____
_____

 Dreams are possible.

My Training Outcomes:

Date: _____

_____
_____
_____
_____
_____
_____
_____
_____
_____
_____
_____
_____
_____
_____
_____

♡ *Flipping out is fun!* ♡

My Training Goals:

Date: _____

_____
_____
_____
_____
_____
_____
_____
_____
_____
_____
_____
_____
_____
_____
_____

Don't give up!

My Training Outcomes:

Date: _____

_____
_____
_____
_____
_____
_____
_____
_____
_____
_____
_____
_____
_____
_____
_____

Train like a champion.

My Competition Goals:

Date: _____

Competition name: _____

_____
_____
_____
_____
_____
_____
_____
_____
_____
_____
_____
_____
_____

COMMENTS: _____
_____

♡ *Trampolining counts as flying.* ♡

My Competition Achievements:

Date: _____

Competition name: _____

_____
_____
_____
_____
_____
_____
_____
_____
_____
_____
_____
_____
_____

SCORES: _____
_____

♡ I love gymnastics! ♡

My Competition Goals:

Date: _____

Competition name: _____

_____
_____
_____
_____
_____
_____
_____
_____
_____
_____
_____
_____

COMMENTS: _____
_____

 If you don't try – you won't know what you're actually capable of.

My Competition Achievements:

Date: _____

Competition name: _____

_____
_____
_____
_____
_____
_____
_____
_____
_____
_____
_____
_____

SCORES: _____
_____

♡ *You got this!* ♡

My Competition Goals:

Date: _____

Competition name: _____

_____
_____
_____
_____
_____
_____
_____
_____
_____
_____
_____
_____

COMMENTS: _____
_____

♡ *Trampolining is the best!* ♡

My Competition Achievements:

Date: _____

Competition name: _____

_____
_____
_____
_____
_____
_____
_____
_____
_____
_____
_____
_____
_____

SCORES: _____

_____

♡ *Don't forget to have fun.* ♡

My Competition Goals:

Date: _____

Competition name: _____

_____
_____
_____
_____
_____
_____
_____
_____
_____
_____
_____
_____
_____

COMMENTS: _____
_____

♡ *Run towards a challenge, not away from it.* ♡

My Competition Achievements:

Date: _____

Competition name: _____

_____
_____
_____
_____
_____
_____
_____
_____
_____
_____
_____
_____
_____

SCORES: _____
_____

♡ *Fly like an eagle.* ♡

My Competition Goals:

Date: _____

Competition name: _____

_____
_____
_____
_____
_____
_____
_____
_____
_____
_____
_____
_____
_____

COMMENTS: _____
_____

♡ *You're amazing.* ♡

My Competition Achievements:

Date: _____

Competition name: _____

_____
_____
_____
_____
_____
_____
_____
_____
_____
_____
_____
_____

SCORES: _____
_____

♡ *Believe – achieve.* ♡

My Competition Goals:

Date: _____

Competition name: _____

_____
_____
_____
_____
_____
_____
_____
_____
_____
_____
_____
_____

COMMENTS: _____
_____

♡ ...it's a gymnast thing. ♡

My Competition Achievements:

Date: _____

Competition name: _____

_____
_____
_____
_____
_____
_____
_____
_____
_____
_____
_____
_____

SCORES: _____
_____

♡ *Be flexible, be strong. And smile!* ♡

My Competition Goals:

Date: _____

Competition name: _____

_____
_____
_____
_____
_____
_____
_____
_____
_____
_____
_____
_____

COMMENTS: _____
_____

 You can do it!

My Competition Achievements:

Date: _____

Competition name: _____

_____
_____
_____
_____
_____
_____
_____
_____
_____
_____
_____
_____
_____

SCORES: _____
_____

Go for gold!

My Competition Goals:

Date: _____

Competition name: _____

_____
_____
_____
_____
_____
_____
_____
_____
_____
_____
_____
_____

COMMENTS: _____
_____

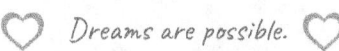 *Dreams are possible.*

My Competition Achievements:

Date: _____

Competition name: _____

_____

_____

_____

_____

_____

_____

_____

_____

_____

_____

_____

_____

SCORES: _____

_____

Flipping out is fun!

My Competition Goals:

Date: _____

Competition name: _____

_____
_____
_____
_____
_____
_____
_____
_____
_____
_____
_____

COMMENTS: _____
_____

♡ *Don't give up!* ♡

My Competition Achievements:

Date: _____

Competition name: _____

_____
_____
_____
_____
_____
_____
_____
_____
_____
_____
_____
_____
_____

SCORES: _____
_____

Train like a champion.

My Competition Goals:

Date: _____

Competition name: _____

_____
_____
_____
_____
_____
_____
_____
_____
_____
_____
_____
_____
_____

COMMENTS: _____
_____

Aim high!

My Competition Achievements:

Date: _____

Competition name: _____

_____

_____

_____

_____

_____

_____

_____

_____

_____

_____

_____

_____

SCORES: _____

_____

♡ *You're a star!* ♡

My Competition Goals:

Date: _____

Competition name: _____

_____
_____
_____
_____
_____
_____
_____
_____
_____
_____
_____
_____

COMMENTS: _____
_____

♡ *Trampolining counts as flying.* ♡

My Competition Achievements:

Date: _____

Competition name: _____

_____
_____
_____
_____
_____
_____
_____
_____
_____
_____
_____
_____

SCORES: _____

_____

I love trampolining!

My Competition Goals:

Date: _____

Competition name: _____

_____
_____
_____
_____
_____
_____
_____
_____
_____
_____
_____
_____
_____
_____

COMMENTS: _____
_____

If you don't try – you won't know what you're actually capable of.

My Competition Achievements:

Date: _____

Competition name: _____

_____
_____
_____
_____
_____
_____
_____
_____
_____
_____
_____
_____

SCORES: _____
_____

 You got this!

My Competition Goals:

Date: _____

Competition name: _____

_____
_____
_____
_____
_____
_____
_____
_____
_____
_____
_____
_____
_____

COMMENTS: _____
_____

♡ *Aim high!* ♡

My Competition Achievements:

Date: _____

Competition name: _____

_____
_____
_____
_____
_____
_____
_____
_____
_____
_____
_____
_____

SCORES: _____
_____

♡ *You're a star!* ♡

My Competition Goals:

Date: _____

Competition name: _____

_____
_____
_____
_____
_____
_____
_____
_____
_____
_____
_____
_____
_____

COMMENTS: _____
_____

♡ *Trampolining counts as flying.* ♡

My Competition Achievements:

Date: _____

Competition name: _____

_____

_____

_____

_____

_____

_____

_____

_____

_____

_____

_____

_____

SCORES: _____

_____

♡ *I love gymnastics!* ♡

My Competition Goals:

Date: _____

Competition name: _____

_____
_____
_____
_____
_____
_____
_____
_____
_____
_____
_____
_____
_____

COMMENTS: _____
_____

♡ *Trampolining is the best!* ♡

My Competition Achievements:

Date: _____

Competition name: _____

_____
_____
_____
_____
_____
_____
_____
_____
_____
_____
_____
_____
_____

SCORES: _____
_____

♡ *Don't forget to have fun.* ♡

My Competition Goals:

Date: _____

Competition name: _____

_____

_____

_____

_____

_____

_____

_____

_____

_____

_____

_____

_____

COMMENTS: _____

_____

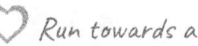 *Run towards a challenge, not away from it.*

My Competition Achievements:

Date: _____

Competition name: _____

_____
_____
_____
_____
_____
_____
_____
_____
_____
_____
_____
_____
_____
_____

SCORES: _____
_____

♡ *Fly like an eagle.* ♡

Extra notes

www.ingramcontent.com/pod-product-compliance
Lightning Source LLC
Chambersburg PA
CBHW070436010526
44118CB00014B/2068